CW01572850

Inchinnan
in old picture postcards

by Wilson Holland

European Library ZALTBOMMEL/THE NETHERLANDS

About the author:

Mr. Wilson Holland, who has studied the local history of his native parish since childhood, was born in Inchinnan main village and he has lived there all his life within 150 yards of the spire of Park Church. He attended the Inchinnan Primary and Renfrew High Schools and in mid-1959 he was a trainee at the National Sea Training School at Sharpness, Gloucestershire, England, for six weeks, whereafter he was in the catering service of the British Merchant Navy Service for a short time.

For the supply of illustrations for this publication Mr. Holland would like to thank the Glasgow University Archives for views 36 to 39 inclusive; The Mitchell Library in Glasgow for view 70; Mr. John F. Anderson of Bishopton for views 6 and 43 and last but not least Mr. Brian Marks of Inchinnan parish church, who so kindly supplied views 3, 47 and 48. And for further information on Inchinnan's early-20th century parish historian Rev. Robert McClelland, see page 10 of the 'Glasgow Evening Citizen' of 4th January 1913.

GB ISBN 90 288 1424 8

© 1999 European Library – Zaltbommel/The Netherlands

Introduction

The 3,300 acre parish of Inchinnan, which is one of the smallest parishes in Scotland, stands upon the southern bank of the river Clyde, eight-and-a-half miles west of the City of Glasgow and three miles north of the Burgh of Paisley. Set in the northeastern part of Renfrewshire its northern section now contains most of 'the new town' of Erskine, which was founded in 1969-1970 and the present population of which now totals some 14,000 persons.

Historically this parish is held to have received its name from the ancient words that denote 'the island of the rivers', a reference to the former island in the Black Cart Water, where the founder of our parish, St. Conval, set up his mission station in 597 A.D. In later ages Inchinnan was to be widely venerated as the burial place of this saint and after his death here in 612 A.D. the site of his original cell at Inchinnan was a centre of pilgrimage until the eve of the Reformation. From 597 until 1965 it was upon the site of St. Conval's original mission station that our various parish churches were to stand, first near to the ford and then near to the two bridges of Inchinnan. Alas! The final kirk on St. Conval's resting place had to be dismantled in 1965-66 due to the transfer of Renfrew Airport to Abbotsinch Aerodrome at Paisley. Its runway was set, by 1960, directly in line with our 'bridges' church, immediately across the river Black Cart. During sixty-one years it stood at Inchinnan Bridge; one

of its former ministers, the late Rev. John I. McBurnie, wrote that the Inchinnan parish church of 1904-1965 was nationally recognized 'as being one of the most beautiful sanctuaries in the Church of Scotland'. On 6th June 1968 the Moderator of the Church of Scotland, Dr. J. B. Longmuir, dedicated our modern Inchinnan kirk at Greenhead Farm in Inchinnan village and the first public worship in this building was held on Sunday, 9th June 1968. In 1997 the 1400th anniversary of the founding of our parish church by St. Conval was celebrated with a number of events organized by its membership. These included a special church service and also a very successful local history exhibition that fully explored the highly fascinating story of our district.

Apart from our various kirk buildings the main features of our parish have been for centuries its country estates, especially those of Park and Southbar and from 1737 the Campbell of Blythswood family lands, but today of these old localities only the romantically wooded Southbar Estate with its in the 1920s renewed house is the only one that comes near to – even if not totally – its old mid-19th century Ordnance Survey Map appearance.

Although there had been some stone quarrying here in the 19th century, and a small-scale coal mining operation between 1865 and 1875 close to Inchinnan Bridge, until 1914 the parish of

Inchinnan had been a purely farming community, which held a population of few hundred persons at most. Then suddenly in 1916, in the middle of the First World War, William Beardmore & Co. founded their huge Inchinnan Airship Construction Works within our parish boundaries and half a mile to the east of it they built the 'Beardmore Cottages' housing scheme, to accommodate some of this factory's 'key workers'. This set of houses were merely the first of several modern public and private housing schemes to be constructed within our district's domains, the bulk of which was finally made to look extremely modest when in 1969-1970 the new township of Erskine burst upon the northern half of our parish.

Some six years after the closing of the Airship Works in 1922, the India Tyre Rubber Factory was opened on its site in July 1928. It rapidly expanded over the decades before its much regretted closure – partly due to modernization problems – in December 1981. It left in its wake its own 1929-30 housing scheme of India Drive and Allans Avenue at its own locality. Then in the mid-1970s the 'Inchinnan Business Park' Industrial Estate gradually emerged close to these homes, a venture which has continually expanded due to its great success in bringing industrial concerns into our parish. In 1931 a now still operating and extended bus garage was opened at Beardmore Cottages. In the 1950s, when I was a schoolboy in this parish, I was happy with it beyond belief, whereas the demolition of All Hallows Church in the mid-1960s saddened me, as I knew so very much of this kirk's remarkable story. Then suddenly in the mid-1960s it was announced that the northern side of our parish was to become the site of the new township of Erskine. The first houses of this new town were built at Bourne Court, Inchinnan, in 1969-70, whilst the first Erskine houses at Bargarran were completed in April 1971. Now, a little over a quarter of a century later, Erskine is a bustling locality that has spread down to our main parish village and eastwards along the south bank of the river Clyde, practically from the site of the old Erskine Ferry, whilst in the other direction this 'new township' has now reached two thirds of the way to Bishopton village. And within the last two or three years Inchinnan parish's last great rural belt of land has been proposed as the site of the vast 'Abbotsholm Industrial Estate' which – if it came into existence – would make the mid-1970s founded 'Inchinnan Business Park' expand all over the southern part of our parish, from the edges of the lands of the Town of Inchinnan Farm at Beardmore Cottages to the Glasgow to Gourock railway line, some two miles westwards to it. Since 1945 the changes in the Inchinnan scene have consistently grown vaster in nature. In 1946, for example, there was a suggestion that the whole Lanarkshire Steel Industry should be moved to Inchinnan! (See 'The Clyde Valley Regional Plan 1946' which was finally printed in 1949.)

If my little work which is presented here should in its own small way recapture any golden memories of a now 'gone-by' Inchinnan district for its readers, then I, as its parish historian, will not have failed them.

Inchinnan, June 1999
Wilson Holland, parish historian

1 According to the 'Breviary of Aberdeen' printed in 1509-10, the founder of our parish – St. Conval – floated across the sea from Ireland to Inchinnan upon a stone in 597 and from his first mission station here – which he founded upon an 'Isle in the River' of the Black Cart Water – he evangelized in Renfrewshire and beyond. St. Conval, who was the son of an Irish king, was in later ages credited with performing a number of miracles. The historian Dr. Alan Macquarrie suggests that the material in the 'Breviary' probably comes from a 'life' of our saint written about 1150. He was buried here in 612 and our parish churches were to be situated on the site of his cell for the next 1,350 years. This delightful representation of St. Conval forms the frontispiece of Rev. Mr. Robert McClelland's splendid 1905 local history monography 'The Church and Parish of Inchinnan'.

ST CONVAL

2   Today surrounded by a sturdy iron fence placed by the 1st Lord Blythswood, the Argyll and St. Conval Stones stand within yards of the 1923 Inchinnan Swing Bridge at Renfrew. The rounded stone is 'The Chariot of St. Conval' on which in 597 this saint is said to have sailed to Inchinnan from Ireland. The second boulder here – originally thought to have been the base of a Celtic cross – is now known as 'The Argyll Stone' due to the fact that the 9th Earl of Argyll was captured near to it during his unsuccessful rebellion in the west of Scotland in 1685. For many centuries the St. Conval Stone was a centre of pilgrimage and cures for the sick were obtained from it by washing this relic with water and bathing the afflicted persons in the liquid that had thus been 'treated'. In the autumn of 1827 Sir Walter Scott, whilst visiting Blythswood House in Renfrew, stated in his diary that 'the Highland drovers are still apt to break Blythswood's fences to see the Argyll Stone'.

3   A remarkably quaint illustration – by a Dutch engraver – of the arrest of the 9th Earl of Argyll at the St. Conval Stones. After his army had broken up he came to Inchinnan ford on 30th June 1685, where after a short struggle some Militia men captured him, he himself muttering the words 'Unfortunate Argyl!' 'The soldiers appeared concerned and some of them even wept when they knew whom they had taken; but they durst not let him go. He was taken to Renfrew and thence to Edinburgh where he died by the axe of the "maiden" as his father had died four and twenty years before.' Possibly Argyll may have been trying to reach Renfrew, where a former tutor to the Argyll family may have been willing to give him both shelter and hiding. It was long believed that many lengthy decades after his detention here, the blood of the Earl was still to be observed upon the 'Argyll Stone' on which he had fallen during his capture.

4 The only known illustration of the 12th century Inchinnan parish church was painted by Mr. Galloway, our parish school headmaster from 1827 until his death in 1866. Built in 1100-1110 the church was at first held by the Knights Templar until 1312 and then by the Knights of St. John until the 1560 Reformation. Writing in 1792 the Rev. Thomas Burns said of its interior: 'A stranger upon entering into it would hardly believe that public worship had been performed in it for a century passed.' Existing for seven centuries with additions and alterations up to 1828, this more than 50 feet long but only 18 feet broad kirk's end is briefly described by the Rev. Mr. Lockhart in his 1836 Statistical Account of Inchinnan, where he states that the area beneath its flooring 'was found to be literally paved with skills' when it was finally removed for the construction of our new 1829-1902 kirk.

5   A memorable view of our parish church of 1829-1902 taken from its adjacent graveyard. In 1836 'owls and other doleful creatures occasionally haunted' its tower. During its existence the parish only had three ministers but they were all of note. The first one, from 1822 to 1860, was Rev. Dr. Lawrence Lockhart, whose eldest brother Mr. J. G. Lockhart was the famous literator and biographer of Sir Water Scott as well as being that writer's son-in-law. The Rev. Dr. Gillan, a celebrated Scottish churchman and the Moderator of the Church of Scotland in 1873-74 was then Inchinnan's minister from 1861 until his death in 1879. In March 1880 our parish historian Rev. Robert McClelland, who had for some time been Dr. Gillan's assistant, was appointed to this church as its twentieth minister after the Reformation.

6 A lovely – if even faded – view of the 1829-1902 Inchinnan Bridge's parish church. In August 1886 this building received choir seats and a Bevington Organ as a gift from the Campbell of Blythswood family. It is hinted in a Glasgow area walkers guide book of 1896 that this organ was the little kirk's pride and joy. These gifts to our congregation were inaugurated by the Reverend of Girvan, Ayrshire, parish church Mr. Corson, whose daughter (1855-1918) was the wife of Robert McClelland, our own parish minister. This lady is commemorated in a stained-glass window that is now modernly placed within our new parish kirk. The Rev. Mr. McClelland (1849-1919), who died in our manse in March 1919, was born in the parish of Girvan. When Mrs. McClelland died in 1918 a local newspaper wrote that her death 'was a loss to the whole district'.

7 The interior of our 1829-1902 church. Before the founding of the 1906 to 1968 Inchinnan 'bridges' church hall, all of the important kirk business meetings were simply held within its confines, as far as I know. In this kirk there were a number of elegantly carved memorials, at least one of which – commemorating the death of Lord Blythswood's younger brother at a canal bridge near Maryhill Glasgow and showing an angel plucking up a water-lily – is now in our modern late-1960s Old Greenock Road sanctuary. In times past – and not so past – an overflowing Black Cart Water has made all of our kirks – plus their manses – indeed 'an island of the rivers' hereabouts. Contemporary designed for its day the views around this little kirk and its grounds were at one time considered to be prettier than those of the English Midlands.

INTERIOR OF LAST CHURCH.
(Built 1828).

8 The 1829-1902 Inchinnan parish kirk as seen from the Black Cart's Abbotsinch bank. Quietly located its picturesque tower contained the kirk bell that stood — forever open to the weather — upon the top of the uncompleted tower of our 1904-1965 kirk. Today it is set — with the 1849 bell of Park Church — within the 75 foot tower of our modern parish kirk. By the mid-1900s the congested and chaotic state of our 'bridges' kirkyard was causing the heritors of our parish concern and it was finally closed for interments — except in a few cases — around 1926. Some two years later on 10 November 1928 our present parish cemetery was opened by the Old Greenock Road above the Broomlands it being jointly dedicated by the Rev. Mr. Stuart of our parish church and the Rev. Mr. Daniel William Macdonald of the Inchinnan United Free Church. In August 1970 this cemetery was under extension.

9 In the late 1890s Lord Blythswood, then Inchinnan's most important landowner, decided to enlarge the 1829 Inchinnan parish church, but it is said it was discovered that its walls could not take the weight of the new parts. What was to become the new 'All Hallows Church' was begun in mid-1899 and it was dedicated in two portions: the first part in April 1902 and the completed building – 'now' with its western transept – in June 1904. This architect's drawing of it has always caused confusion amongst researchers of this building, as it appears that there was a plan to erect a smaller square tower at the 1904 kirk's western end. However, this sketch shows in fact the tower (and the lower walls) of the early 19th century Inchinnan kirk that was subsequently removed (an alteration to the original plan) in 1902 for the purpose of the total renewal of this sanctuary.

10   In June 1904 the opening of All Hallows Church – Inchinnan's third kirk since 1100 – brought such great crowds of viewers that the Rev. Mr. McClelland had to give orders for the kirk's outside gate to be kept locked! The gift to our parish of the 1st Lord Blythswood (1837-1908) of Blythswood House Renfrew, in thanks the Kirk Session of the church on behalf of the people of Inchinnan presented the Illuminated Address shown here to Lord Blythswood. Sadly – with the death of the last Lord Blythswood on active military service during the Second World War – this family line is now no more. It has long been claimed that Robert Burn's 'Bonnie Lass of Ballochmyle', who died in Glasgow in 1843 and whose burial place is unknown, lies buried in the ancient Inchinnan parish graveyard where All Hallows Church stood until 1965. Certainly at that date the Alexanders of the Ballochmyle family owned our parish's Southbar Estate.

ILLUMINATED ADDRESS TO LORD BLYTHSWOOD,
ON THE DEDICATION OF ALL-HALLOWS CHURCH, INCHINNAN.

11   The eastern front of All Hallows Church 'rising like a great sea cliff' as it was viewed from its adjoining kirk grounds. This kirk's tower – finally circa 70 feet – was never raised to the intended 125 foot height and the reasons given for this were 'shortage of funds' (the forever 'celebrated' explanation!), 'the kirk's weak foundations couldn't take the completed tower's weight', 'Lord Blythswood thought he had spent enough on the building already' or 'thought that the tower looked all right without being finished'. However, I understand that when Lord Blythswood died in July 1908 his finances were divided between two sections of his family and neither of these ever came forward with the funds to complete the sanctuary. Some sixty years later the Ministry of Aviation – in view of the development of Abbotsinch Airport in Paisley as the City of Glasgow's new airport – paid some £135,000 to the Church of Scotland in compensation for the kirk's demolition.

12 The vestry porch of our 1904-1965 church. From just below ground level beside its highly ornate staircase, the kirk's boiler house was set – and sometimes rain-flooded! – and above it the kirk's vestry room containing a large fireplace with a framed copy of the famous painting of the 'The Last Supper' set upon the wall above it. Also displayed in here were Mr. Galloway's paintings of our 1100 kirk, an exterior view of our 1829 church and a sketch of the original late-1890s extension plan for our 1820s kirk. Above this room – and reached at step sixteen on the fifty-nine step spiral staircase to the room beneath the top of the kirk's tower – was lo- cated the kirk's organ room (or chamber) wherein the works of this church's organ, which is still in use in our 1968 building, were located.

An ever favourite hobby of the younger generation, when within this room, was to write their names in pencil upon the black-painted boards which guarded the works of the organ from the curious who wished to explore this 'chamber's' depths.

13 The western transept of our 1904-1965 kirk with the Rev. Mr. McClelland standing at its west porch. Upon this transept's site stood our 1829-1902 church and the picturesque stone flight of steps seen in this view gave our 1904 building a sweeping approach. Located beneath floor level at this transept's western terminal was the Blythswood family burial vault which had once been a part of our 1828-1902 kirk. It was entered by an outside porchway, much of which was removed in 1967. This porch had the words 'I dwell amongst my own people' inscribed above its doorway. Above this burial vault, set in the kirk's walls, was its western transept's great rose window which could be breathtaking to observe from the inside when the sun was sinking to the west beyond its shading exterior trees.

14 The interior of the western transept of our 1904-1965 kirk. Here some of the kirks fine wooden pews can be seen, the Blythswood memorial plaque and above it the church's exquisite great western rose window – its stained glass covered with the faces of angels – all of which are now in our new building. Unfortunately it was not possible to save this transept's great beam roof of which all wooden supports individually weighed two-and-a half tons. Upon this transept's northern wall were placed the two parish's world war memorial tablets which were – and still are – in our new village kirk accompanied by an unusually designed electric lamp. These tablets record the names of nineteen parishioners who died in the First World War and of seven in the Second. Also at our new kirk are the two small but delightful stained glass windows from All Hallows Church that illustrate St. Conval and Glasgow's patron saint, St. Mungo.

INTERIOR OF ALL-HALLOWS
(Viewed from the Chancel).

15   A striking view from across the Black Cart Water of our 1904-1965 church which was designed by Sir Robert Rowand Anderson. He also worked on restoring Dunblane Cathedral, Paisley Abbey, Iona Cathedral, and many other projects, but it is alleged that Lord Blythswood – in private – referred to him as 'Ruin' Anderson due to the (reported) £20,000 cost of All Hallows and also that he advised others not to use him because of his expensive ideas! However, Sir Robert did attend Lord Blythswood's funeral service in this kirk in July 1908. But despite the fame of its architect and the beauty of its 15th century Gothic architecture which caused some to call it 'a miniature cathedral', All Hallows Church was generally speaking only 'known' locally.

Inchinnan Parish Church, Manse.

16 All Hallows Church was always a difficult building to photograph 'in one go' and here is a 1900s picture postcard maker's 'attempt' to do as much as possible of it. Abbotsinch Airport was founded in the early 1930s and by the time the Royal Navy had left it, this airport's runway was in direct line with our parish church's tower over which there was only a sixteen feet air space gap between it and any aircraft passing over – hence the kirk's mid-1960s demolition. Some Saturday afternoons in the latter 1950's I would visit, with the rest of the local Boy Scouts, the top of this tower, where there were no fences to guard its circa 16 foot diameter area.

The only thing to do for the fearful was to hang on to the timber supports that stood around the kirk's bell! This bell was rang via a rope in the practically empty room beneath the tower's topmost height which was lit by the eight rose windows – two in each wall – that were such a notable feature of this structure's upper walls.

Parish Church.

Inchinnan

"Scottish Series" G. T. & S. G.

17   The ancient carved stones of Inchinnan graveyard have been of great interest to Scottish antiquarians for generations. Fully noted by both their past and present publications, these Celtic and Templar gravestones – some said to be now around 1,200 years old – are placed in our new 1968 church's grounds. Covered with faded carvings a particularly highly decorated one may once have marked out the grave of St. Conval himself. For countless centuries totally neglected and ignored at our 'bridges' graveyard they were by 1910 at last receiving the attention they fully deserved. In July 1926 it was reported that three of these stones had been made ancient monuments. In an old publication of about 1895, 'The Paisley Portfolio', it is stated that some of the carved stones were removed 'to the Antiquarian Museum Edinburgh', but I understand that this claim has never been verified by any later investigator.

18 The 'age' of the Manse of Inchinnan which was demolished at 'the bridges' in the autumn of 1955 is uncertain but it appears to have been built in the 1820s. Locally it is held 'to have contained 21 rooms – some of them box rooms'. In 1827 the parish church manse here was visited by Sir Walter Scott to meet his son-in-law Mr. J. G. Lockhart, who was our kirk minister's eldest brother. In June 1955 in an article in the 'Renfrewshie Gazette' the Rev. Mr. McBurnie stated that Sir Walter visited the actual manse that he (Mr. McBurnie) himself was now occupying. However, the same year Mr. McBurnie also informed the Presbytery of Paisley that this edifice was in such a deplorable condition that he refused 'to stay another winter in it' and 'Friarscroft' our Renfrew 'temporary manse' – latterly from 1955 to 1969 – was purchased soon afterwards.

MANSE OF INCHINNAN.

19 Inchinnan Manse and kirk about 1930. When our manse was demolished here in the autumn of 1955 there was no indication that by about 1960 a proposal to transfer Renfrew Airport's operations to Paisley's Abbotsinch Airport would mean the end of All Hallows Church and its church hall. By mid-1961 a question mark hung over all our church properties and finally, after protracted negociations with the Church of Scotland and the relevent authorities, it was agreed to erect a modern kirk one mile away at Inchinnan main village. All Hallows was removed in 1965-66 and some of its fittings were stored for transferral to our new building, which was opened in June 1968. Ladyacre Cottage 'went' in 1967 and our 'bridges' church hall of 1906 was removed by the end of 1968.

Very unfortunately a proposal to have Lord Blythswood's church moved stone-by-stone to a new site was never acted upon.

20 Born near Hawick in October 1800 Rev. Dr. Gillan was one of Scotland's greatest 19th-century preachers. Licensed by the Presbytery of Selkirk in 1829 he served in six ministerial charges before he came to Inchinnan in January 1861. The crowning glory of his life came in 1873 when he was appointed Moderator of the Church of Scotland and it is recorded in his 'Renfrewshire Gazette' obituary that 'In the movement for the building of the Wallace Monument he keenly participated and he spoke elegantly and vigorously at its inauguration on the Abbey Craig at Stirling'. In October 1870 the City of Glasgow presented him with his portrait and amongst other items they gifted a diamond ring to Mrs. Gillan. When he died in the Manse of Inchinnan in November 1879 his congregation met on the following Sunday in our parish church, but the usual service was disposed with and after engaging in appropriate worship and prayer they dismissed themselves.

RT. REV. DR. GILLAN.

21 Born in the parish of Girvan, Ayrshire, on 7th July 1849 Rev. Robert McClelland served our parish kirk for 39 years until his death on 1st March 1919. Our parish minister from March 1880, in July 1882 he married Miss Corson (1855-1918), the daughter of the minister of Girvan parish church, and they had a family of three sons. In 1900 Mr. McClelland was sent to South Africa as a chaplain to the forces fighting in the Boer War and returning home he spoke widely about his wartime experiences. In 1902 he wrote about it in his work 'Heroes and Gentlemen'. 'An expert on all things about Inchinnan' by 1896, he was engaged by 1902 in writing our parish history which finally appeared in 1905, published by Alexander Gardner of Paisley. Mr. McClelland also wrote a book on beekeeping.

22   Delighted with the 1904 Inchinnan parish church of Lord Blythswood it was Rev. Mr. McClelland's sad duty to officiate, together with the Rev. Mr. Macdonald of our Free Church, at Lord Blythswood's funeral service in July 1908. At the start of the First World War in 1914 two of Mr. McClelland's sons are known to have served at the front, one being killed in the Gallipoli Campaign in June 1915, whilst his second son – a military padre – was badly gassed at the front in 1918. Later this son was to be the minister of Dollar parish church from 1920 to 1928 and then until his death in May 1931 the minister of Burnside parish church in Glasgow. When Rev. Mr. McClelland deceased on 1st March 1919 'The Renfrew Press' reported 'that although Mr. McClelland had been in failing health for some time' (he had applied for an assistant and successer only a short time before) 'his death had come as a shock to some members of his congregation'.

THE REVEREND ROBERT M'CLELLAND.

23　For a long time Inchinnan Bridge together with the towers of the 19th and 20th century churches of Inchinnan were close to classic landmarks on the Glasgow to Gourock highway. Although – far more often passed by than visited – anyone who came off this roadway found – until the mid-1960s – a delightful spot of peace 'and rare beauty' within our kirk grounds. This locality is one of the oldest church sites in Scotland having been founded by St. Conval in 597, where the churches of Inchinnan were destined to stand for over 1,350 years until 1965. For centuries the kirk stood near the famous river ford at Inchinnan whilst their own locality overshadowing it was venerated as a place of pilgrimage right up to the eve of the 1560 Reformation. The first Inchinnan Bridge of 1759 collapsed in 1809 due to a floodtide on the rivers it crossed – its 'cheap and nasty' mid-18th century construction work being blamed for its destruction.

24   Similar to the original Inchinnan Bridge of 1759-1809 a toll charge had to be resorted again to pay off the building costs of the new 1812 road bridge. This new bridge's toll house stood for long facing the junction of the Greenock and Paisley roads until its demolition in December 1931. In November 1912 a massive flood on the rivers submerged this house's lowest parts by several feet – thus causing great distress to its occupants. A few signs of this toll house's lower ground level foundations – plus a cold empty 'room' part of it under this bridge's roadway – still mark out its old locality. Constructed at a cost of £17,000 this 187 year old bridge was formed out of stone from Mr. Fulton's quarry in the Park Estate where a large part of Erskine New Town has been erected since 1969-70.

The Bridges, Inchinnan, Renfrew.

25 Inchinnan Bridge's Black Cart span. This structure of 1809-1812, which is set at a right angle over the two rivers it originally passed across, meets in its centre the Abbots-inch-Paisley roadway and then with its shorter and now dry land beneath White Cart Bridge it connects with the Inchinnan Swing Bridge. For long a favourite subject for artists to paint it is still in daily use, taking a weight of traffic for which it was never designed. As Rev. Robert McClelland wrote of it in 1905: 'It reflects the utmost credit alike on trustees, architect (Robertson Buchanan), and builder.' In 1891 due to navigational improvements on the adjoining White Cart River its foundations were weakened and the present line of planks just set downstream from it were put in place soon after at a cost of £207 17s. At low tide on the river these planks form a 'waterfall' that was in rainy weather once known as 'the falls of Cart'.

Inchinnan Stone Bridge, Renfrew.

26 A view that powerfully illustrates the immense size of the 1812 Inchinnan stone bridge as it towers above the Black Cart Water. In 1812 it was reported that its foundations reached to forty feet beneath the bottom of the rivers it crossed. Once there was a boathouse near Inchinnan Manse and it was possible to row up the river Black Cart to the Walkinshaw Estate some two miles upstream, just beyond the Barnsford Bridge. By 1927 Bridge Island was with its growing collection of small sailing craft, being compared with the boating scene on Loch Lomond. There also was a small Renfrew Sea Scout within our 'bridges' parish church grounds In the final decade before All Hallows kirk's removal. One Saturday afternoon around 1950, whilst I and my family were rowing downstream, we were momentarily jammed by riverbed stones and by the time we had worked ourselves free, we were being watched by a group of 'interested spectators' from this bridge!

Stane Brig.   *Inchinnan.*

27   In order to improve the navigation of the White Cart Water to Paisley in 1790 a canal was cut at Blythswood – then known as Renfield – to ease the river's problems for the little craft that used it. This operation formed the present Bridge Island. Records suggest that there were three swing bridges across the canalised part of the river White Cart at Inchinnan Bridge between 1792 and about 1920. The first seemingly lasted till 1835 when a Clyde to Paisley river improvement led to its replacement. Again renewed in 1876 the third bridge shown here survived – finally totally outmoded – until about 1920, when it was removed for the construction of the present early 1920s Inchinnan Swing Bridge structure. By this lifting bridge there stands upon its Bridge Island side the former swing bridge's keeper's cottage. In 1865 its predecessor here consisted of a square thatch-roofed white-washed cottage.

Swing Bridge, Renfrew.

28   Constructed in 1876 this little – but vital – swing bridge over the White Cart river at Inchinnan survived, despite complaints from road users about its condition and from the Paisley shipbuilders about its waterway obstructing capacities, until it was replaced in 1921-23 by the present huge Arrol & Co. built swing bridge that now occupies its site. In November 1880 a horse and waggon load of straw – from Mr. Gilmuir's Town of Inchinnan farm – was completely blown into the river northwards from this mid-1870s structure – 'the driver (but not the horse or cart) just escaping in the very nick of time'. As its railings were too low, damages were recovered from the responsible highway authorities by Mr. Gilmuir for the loss of both his horse and vehicle. These totaled £105 plus expenses. The Rev. Mr. McClelland records that he was personally at this swing bridge within minutes of the accident taking place.

THE SWING BRIDGE, RENFREW.

29 An important day in Clydeside transportation history occurred on Wednesday, 28th March 1923, when the present Inchinnan Swing Bridge was opened at Kirklandneuk, Renfrew. This was a widely acknowledged event. Its construction broadened the White Cart's channel at 'the bridges' from 48 feet to 90 feet. This bridge, still in operation today, cost some £62,000 to complete and in February 1936 it was reported that it 'was only raised 20 times a week' to allow shipping to proceed to and from Paisley Harbour. But with this harbour's closure in the mid-1960s it is now almost 'an event' to see this bridge raised for any reason. And whilst it appears to be locally speaking massive, in the mid-1920s 'The Renfrew Press' newspaper reported that a passing American tourist had been heard boasting that some USA children played with Meccano sets that were larger than it!

OPENING CEREMONY OF INCHINNAN BRIDGE, WED. 28TH MARCH, 1923.

30 A splendid 1930s Valentines of Dundee postcard of the Arrol & Co. White Cart Swing Bridge a mile west of Renfrew, one of the best known highway landmarks in western central Scotland. Arrols & Co. signed the contract to build it in May 1921. Until 1759 the conjoint mouth of the White and Black Cart rivers near here were traversed by a long celebrated river fording and ferrying place – often mentioned in old charters – which once had a two-storey house and inn close by, run by one Sanders Muir. Interestingly some very slight signs of the original ten-arch mid-18th century bridge at Inchinnan lie just visible in the Black Cart's riverbed just north of the now almost 190 years old stone roadway bridge which replaced it in the early 19th century. Mr. J. G. Lockhart, Sir Walter Scott's biographer, stated that the view northwards from Inchinnan Bridge was one of the finest that he had ever seen.

SWING BRIDGE, RENFREW.

A.3851.

31 Bridge Island – today the base of the Inchinnan Cruising Club, founded in 1932 – was formed in the 1790s by the half mile navigational canal over which the present 1923 Inchinnan Swing Bridge lies. This channel was partly constructed because of the difficulty of sailing ships getting their masts beneath the arches of the first Inchinnan Bridge of 1759-1809. This bridge was remarkable as it ran straight across the rivers with the Paisley road coming in – finally 'bridgewise' – to meet its southern central part in the middle of the two streams – and therefore it boasted of three entry and exit roadways to and from it. In March 1931 Mr. James Fyfe, the Blythswood Estate factor, stated he would accept £150 for the 1812 bridge's Toll House if this obstruction to modern traffic was immediately removed – as it was the following December.

Today almost all of the old rural charm of Inchinnan Bridge has completely vanished.

Meeting of the Waters, Renfrew

32 Inchinnan Road, Renfrew, in the 1900s, showing a quaint serenity that it has long since lost. One mile long to Inchinnan Kirk's original site it had still until relatively recent decades two little lodge houses in its northern environments, that until the early 1930s guarded the entry lanes to Blythswood House, one of Renfrewshire's greatest mansion houses, which was for long the home of the Campbell of Blythswood family. Finished in 1820 its contents were auctioned off in 1929 and this large building was finally removed in 1934-35. In the early 1900s its occupant, Lord Blythswood, who had been raised to the Peerage in 1892, was the owner of several still well-known farming and agricultural properties in our parish. Many years ago Inchinnan Road's potholed unsurfaced roadway constantly taxed the energies of the 'new-fangled' motor cars of the early 20th century.

Inchinnan Rd. Renfrew.

33 The Battle of Renfrew fought in 1164 between King Malcolm IV and Somerled Lord of the Isles is said to have taken place around the area of Inchinnan's Newshot Island and the much later site of the Teucheen ('Chugheen') Wood which stands today behind Beardmore Cottages. Commemorated in a 'curious rhyming Latin poem' local tradition claims that it was at 'The Blood Mires Goat' – just behind Florish Farm, today occupied by the Dick family – where the worst of the fighting took place. The history of Scotland relates that the King won this fight and that Somerled was slain. Parishwise it was long claimed that two old mounds within the Teucheen Wood formed the graves of those slain in the conflict. Still extant apparently no antiquities of any description were found in them when they were utilised from the 1890s to 1941 by the Blythswood family for a privately managed gravitational water supply system.

THE FIELD OF RENFREW

34 Inchinnan's first modern housing scheme, Beardmore Cottages, came in 1916-17 when William Beardmore & Co. founded upon the lands of Allans Farm the Inchinnan Airship Construction Works. 'The cottages' as they are known locally consist of some fifty or so homes near the Teucheen Wood and are still occupied today. During the Clydeside blitz in March 1941 some of them had their whole window frames – but not the small glass panes in them – blown in when the greenhouses at Florish Farm were bombed. This mid-1920s view of 'the cottages' has now vanished as in early 1931 the present Inchinnan Bus Garage was partly placed in front of them by the Ferguson 'Victoria' Bus Co., who were amongst the pioneers of the Gourock-Glasgow bus route. In 1932 this garage became a base for the Western S.M.T. bus service.

35   The Town of Inchinnan Farm in 1913 which stands modernly opposite Beardmore Cottages. In January 1843 this farm was the scene of a once celebrated murder case, when its tenant Mr. John Gilmuir died in controversial circumstances. His wife, the former Christina Cochran of Dunlop in Ayrshire, was arrested in New York after sailing the Atlantic and was finally brought to trial in Edinburgh in January 1844 – after being held for four months in Paisley Prison. A verdict of 'Not Proven' was returned. She died aged 87 at Stewarton Ayrshire in December 1905, roughly three months after Robert McClelland (who makes no mention of this case) had issued our parish history. One of the judges at the trial also presided over the much better known murder trial of Glasgow's Madeleine Smith. An old Inchinnan gentleman told me that the first time he had ever seen a compass being used it was being carried by an Ayrshire man 'who wanted to see the farm where John Gilmuir had died'.

36 The Inchinnan Airship shed, measuring 720 feet long, 230 feet at its base and 122 feet high, was built at Allans Farm between January and September 1916. It had huge doors at both ends that took 13 minutes to open, which were guarded on their Greenock Road side by two windscreens of 700 feet long and 60 feet high. Owned by Wm. Beardmore & Co. this factory's first airship, No. 24, was built for reconnaisance purposes and she made her first flight here on 21st July 1917. Her girders had been manufactured at Dalmuir and then transported to Inchinnan. By the end of 1918 her serviceability was questionable because of her gas-bags and envelope durability. 535 feet long and with a diameter of 53 feet she was left in a mooring experiment, 'afixed' to a tower at Pulham Norfork England for some time in 1919, where she managed to survive both rain and high winds. Attempts to land her by rope, however, were not very successful. After this 1919 experiment the No. 24 airship was demolished.

37   Inchinnan's second airship was the R27. 539 feet 3 inches long with a diameter of 53 feet she was owned by the Royal Navy who planned to use her for reconnaisance work. 'Laid down' in mid-March 1917 she was completed in April 1918 and she had her maiden flight in June 1918. A '23X' type of airship of which two were built in Great Britain, it had an internal walking corridor within her hull. Powered by four Rolls Royce engines with eighteen gas bags she was an easily constructed vessel which had been designed by C.I.R. Campbell, who was to die in the R38 airship disaster over the river Humber in August 1921. On 16th August 1918 the R27 was to be destroyed in an airship hangar fire at Howden in Yorkshire. Within her brief lifespan she had logged 90 hours of flying time.

38 Inchinnan's 'great' airship was the 643 feet long and 78 feet 9 inches in diameter R34. Completed in March 1919 she made a 56-hour flight along the North German coast and over the Baltic Sea between 17th and 20th June 1919. Earlier, on 9th May 1919, she had been inspected at Inchinnan by Sir Douglas Haig, Britain's famous First World War commander. In July 1919 she became widely celebrated as the first aerial craft to make a double crossing of the Atlantic to the United States and back, starting from East Fortune airfield near Edinburgh. However, this trip was a near disaster because of her 'inadequate design' and a fuel shortage on its outward leg which left the U.S. Navy 'half expecting' to have to tow it in from the sea – at least! In his 1984 book 'Airships-Cardington' Mr. Geoffrey Chamberlain writes (page 88): 'This was only one of several British airship flights which hindsight has shown ought to never have been made.' In January 1921, after 500 hours of flight, the R34 was seriously damaged in a collision with a hillside in Yorkshire. Then, on limping back to her base, she was immediately scrapped.

39 Inchinnan's final airship (two other orders for the '28' and R40 having been cancelled in 1917 and 1919 respectively) was the gigantic R36 which measured 672 feet 2 inches long and 78 feet 9 inches in diameter. 'Out' of her shed in April 1921 she was able to carry fifty passengers plus a crew of 28. Costing £350,000 she was accidentally damaged when she overshot a mooring mast at Pulham Market Norfork two months after launching and despite having been partially reconditioned for £13,500 she was never to fly again, and was kept in a shed until she was finally demolished in 1925. She had flown for around 80 hours. Despite the gas bags having been made here for the English-built R38, the Inchinnan Airship Construction Works were disposed of in December 1922 and the Arrol & Co.-built airship shed was demolished in 1923, with explosives being used to bring part of it down. A neighbouring airship factory shed – which later became a part of the India Tyres factory – remained here until it was finally removed in June 1984.

40 Five years after the closing of our airship works its site was taken over by the India Tyre Rubber Co. Ltd. Opened in July 1928 this works operated here until December 1981, when it was closed down. Today only its office block by the Glasgow to Greenock A8 highway – plus the late 1920s homes in India Drive and Allands Avenue near to it that were built to house some of its workers – remain. A huge Beardmore Airship Factory shed at the back of it, latterly well seen from Abbotsinch Airport Paisley – which had been a First World War aircraft hangar and later a motor car tyre storage place – was finally demolished in June 1984. At times this structure has been wrongly identified as the shed (in fact removed in 1923) where our four airships were constructed. The India Tyre factory's 'brand' of motor car wheel tyres were widely known amongst both drivers and vehicle accessory salesmen throughout the United Kingdom. This is 'The Tyres Work' in 1929-1930.

41   The India Tyres factory from the air in 1949. Near to it, on its India Drive-Allans Avenue side, was – and in 1999 still is – its large recreation ground. The 'India Tyres Gala Day' that was yearly held upon it was forever a massive crowd puller. This field's sports pavillion was opened in August 1934 at a cost of £800. A film of the 1936 India Tyres Sports Day was shown at the Picture House in Paisley. Needless to say our parish was widely known because of the 'India of Inchinnan' works and its office block was in later times floodlit at night. Its first manager, Mr. Andrew Melville, once owned the island of Inchmurrin in Loch Lomond which he had purchased from the Duke of Montrose. In a 'Paisley Daily Express' article of 24th July 1996 it is stated that this works once employed 1,200 men. Since its closure in December 1981 the 'regular features' of this factory, such as the sounding of 'the three o'clock horn', have been widely missed locally.

42 The present Northbar House – once known as 'The House of Hill' – was erected in c. 1741 on a hilly bluff above the former main Greenock road through our parish. When Mr. M'Gilchrist sold most of his Northbarr Estate around 1740 he retained a wing of it and constructed this house as his new residence. Inchinnan's original 'Northbarr House ' – once a Semple family possession which stood close to the Erskine Ferry – vanished roughly about 1830-1840. The 1740s Northbar House – once the laundry of the Blythswood family – was reached from the Old Greenock Road through 'Duncan's Gate' – now forty years gone – which was named long ago after an occupant of this mansion. Once its site was occupied by the Preceptory of Greenend where the Knights Templar and Knights of St. John lived, and Mr. McClelland writes 'there can be little doubt that some of the sacred stones of the old fabric were incorporated into the new building'.

43 The Broomlands hamlet and its accompanying Park Church and – perhaps lesser so – the Luckingsford row of houses close by were for a long time landmarks on and near the Old Greenock Road. A picturesque set of houses but finally totally inadequate for more modern times the Broomlands at one time contained a local post office shop that was lastly run, until about 1954 in a part of the former smithy house, by the late Miss Margaret Earl. This small hamlet, together with the Luckingsford nearby, was for decades the principal population centre of our parish. The Broomlands is said to have received its name from the amount of Broom plants that once grew near it, whilst the Luckingsford probably received it name from the fact that its locality once looked towards the former river ford at Inchinnan kirk. In 1905 there were in the parish a postal telegraph office, a village library, a Penny Savings Bank and a Dorcas Society at the Broomlands.

44 The Broomlands itself. The large nearest house here was its smithy house and like its lower conjoint former blacksmith's shop it still exists today. The two-storied house that adjoined the smithy lasted till about 1949, but the central parts of these dwelling houses vanished – as did all of the nearby Luckingsford houses – in the mid-1930s, when the first homes were constructed in the Luckingsford Renfrewshire County Council housing scheme immediately behind Park Church. The easternmost cottage seen here finally vanished, like its long time accompanying tree, in March 1994. Today two sets of 1970s and mid-1990s flats occupy most of the Broomlands original site and this old parish place name is hardly ever used for any purpose in our district any more. In the 1850s Mr. John Henderson of Park House Inchinnan – 'with others' – owned the houses in the Broomlands.

BROOMLANDS, INCHINNAN.

45 The western terminus of the Broomlands houses looking to the field where Broomlea Crescent was formed in 1947-48. In August 1880 Queen Victoria, who was then at Blythswood House, drove from Paisley to the Barnsford Bridge and through our parish departing over Inchinnan Bridge. In a book published in Paisley in 1917 it is recorded that 'At the village of Inchinnan a warm welcome was accorded to Her Majesty'. The old Luckingsford houses were on 'Rennies Road' a rough farm track that is named after the occupants of the now vanished Freeland Farm that stood on it, about one mile west of our village. Shortly, near this lane's north-eastern side the new East Freeland private housing scheme will be found, which was begun in April 1999, despite a previous unsuccessful legal attempt to have its construction prevented on the contention that its proposed site was a haven for natural life.

Broomlands Village, near Renfrew.

46 Park Church Inchinnan, which was opened in October 1849, was constructed for the 1843 formed Inchinnan Free Church congregation by Mr. John Henderson of Park, Esq. Until 1859 it was served by various preachers, including Rev. William Govan, who founded the Lovedale Missionary Institute in South Africa and who is today looked upon as one of the great educationalists of the 19th century. From 1859 its ministers were Rev. Mr. Cruickshank (1859-1863), Rev. Mr. M'Turk (1864-1891), Rev. Mr. M'Lean (1891-99) and Rev. Daniel William Macdonald (1899-1933). After Mr. Macdonald's death it was first linked to our parish church in 1934 and then finally united with it four years later. Closed in mid-1968 it has been a church hall since autumn 1970. Its now privately owned former manse dating from 1860, seen here behind it, was also built by Mr. Henderson, who laid this church's foundation stone in July 1849.

47 Park Church's interior set out for a harvest Thanksgiving service of many years ago. In 1901 it became the United Free Church of Inchinnan and in 1906 two local gentlemen paid for its internal re-decoration and this, in the words of a 'Renfrewshire Gazette' report, 'made it one of the most comfortable churches in the district'. In 1929 the union of the United Free Church with the Church of Scotland led to many congregations uniting. Park Church's membership was forever small and despite its opposition after the death of its last minister in 1933, and a hearing on the matter by the Synod of Clydeside in April 1934, it was at first linked to our parish church on 10th June 1934 under its minister Rev. Mr. Sawyer and then finally united with it on 10th July 1938. Until 1968 the parish church's Sunday morning service was held at our 'bridges' kirk whilst our Sunday evening service (now discontinued) was held in Park Church.

48 The Park Church pulpit area as it was before its closure in June 1968. Today it is a second hall for our parish church's use. In 1958 a harmonium which was set within its pews near to its pulpit was replaced by the organ shown, that after its disuse in 1968 was transferred to the Kirk of Traquair in Peeblesshire. This edifice which could seat 150 persons received some damage from the great Glasgow area gale of January 1968 and in 1979 a tall chimney that stood above its little vestry was removed for safety reasons, whilst its roof was also re-slated at this time at a cost of £2,500. Its Communion Table and Chair – presented by the Adam family of Barnhill Farm Inchinnan in 1949 – is now in our modern kirk at Greenhead Farm. This delightful little edifice of 1849 with its charming little spire has been a local landmark for the last 150 years.

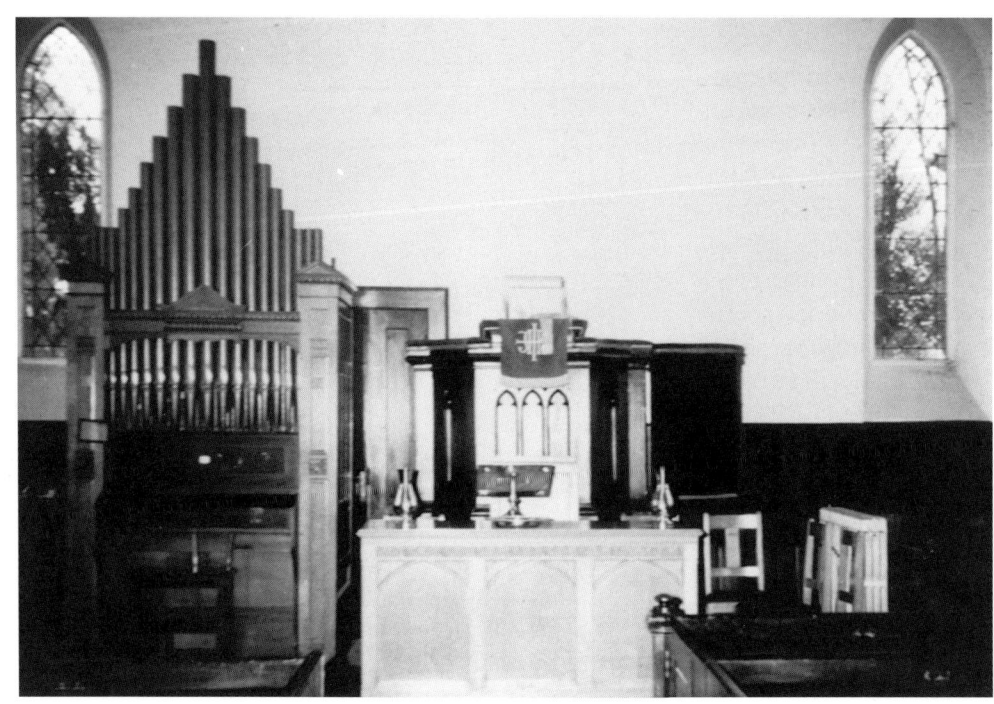

49   Park Church's most famous preacher was Principal Robert Rainy (1826-1906), who was 'to rise high' within the Free, later United Free Church of Scotland. He served in the Free Church College in Edinburgh and it was under his vision and statesmanship that in 1900 the Free Church and the United Presbyterian Church finally united to form the United Free Church of Scotland. He served at Park Church from March to September 1850 and an old member of these times later recalled Mr. Rainy 'as "a bonnie lad", but she had little to say about his pulpit abilities!' Rev. Daniel W. Macdonald reported to his congregation during a pulpit reference to this gentleman on his death in December 1906. Three books (at least) were written on his life. It is a testimony to the former membership of this kirk that for many years (even after 1968) a framed photograph of Principal Rainy hung on a wall of the vestry of Park Church.

PRINCIPAL RAINY.

50   Our former schoolhouse was built by our local ancestors close to the Broomlands between 1827 and 1830. Three of its occupants were the late Mr. Buchanan (headmaster here from December 1912 until June 1938), Mr. James MacIntyre (1939-1953) and Mr. James Steele (1953-1976). In 1935-36 our new parish school was built near to it and this former two-roomed 1830s school was turned into its present gymnasium. In March 1968 the schoolhouse itself was removed and its large garden area now forms the site of the Inchinnan Community Centre's Bowling Green, opened in April 1988 . Mr. Buchanan's son informed me that this edifice's long familar blank window was a result of the window tax! A former headmaster, Mr. Crawford, always considered himself to be the youngest of 'The Old Parochials' as he was appointed to Inchinnan school one day before the 1872 Education Act came into force. Unfortunately he was to be one of the most seriously injured when the 'half crown stand' collapsed at Paisley Racecourse in August 1902, but he still served here until 1909.

51 Although taken as recently as September 1964 there are many changes to be spotted in this view of 'the corner, Inchinnan'. Wilson's expanded smallholding is now hidden amongst the Bourne Court housing scheme and a single tree to the right of it – just outside this picture – was, until it was removed in August 1999, set very inconspicuously amidst the back courts of these fashionable homes. Most people will recall how local children played amongst its branches when all was green around it. It is claimed that the original Bourne Court housing development which was completed at 'the corner' in 1969-70 is – from the planning to its final building stages – the first residential property in Great Britain to be entirely constructed through the use of the metric measurements system. Today the more modern sections of Bourne Court's private housing developments spread out from here both northwards and westwards to edge upon Erskine's Newshot Drive.

52   Like the vast marjority of our local place names Freeland Farm – on 'Rennies Road' about a mile west of our main village – has been known for hundreds of years. In his 1710 History of Renfrewshire George Crawfurd records that 'the lands of Freeland' (were) 'the inheritance of the Stewarts of Kilecroy in olden times, and now the property of William Maxwell of Freeland, brother to the Laird of Dargevel'. In 1782 Semple adds: 'The lands of Freeland (comprehending Lukensford) are a fine fertile soil, having a good slatehouse two stories high, with good orchards and gardens, (only the garden-walls as yet excepted); at the south-east side is a pleasant little plot of planting adjoining the garden'. And today? Freeland Farm, like the farms of Bargarran, Park Mains, Garnieland, Craigend and the lands of Rashielee, have all fallen victim to the ever increasing size of Erskine within our ancient parish.

53   The farmhouse of Garnieland Farm – the fields of which are now covered with Erskine housing – vanished some time after July 1979. Garnieland's one great claim to fame was that it stood close to the Palace of Inchinnan, an ancient edifice that was visited at least once by James IV of Scotland. In ruins by 1710 it had totally vanished by 1782 as its last surviving remains had been used to repair the gable of the adjacent farmhouse. Even in 1836 some local people could recall viewing a part of it. In 1941 Garnieland Farm witnessed the two nights of the 'Clydebank Blitz' as that Burgh was just opposite across the river Clyde. A much more welcome Clydebank subject seen from here – and elsewhere locally too – was 'Singers' (sewing machine factory) Clock' – which was the largest timepiece in Europe and the second largest one in the world. Unfortunately this feature of Clydebank's scenescape was demolished in April 1963, whereas this whole factory was finally closed in June 1980.

54   Park House stood one third of a mile north of Park Church on land now occupied by Erskine's 1996-1998 'Riverpark' private housing scheme. Constructed about 1780 by a family of the name of Campbell this pleasant looking building of around twenty rooms was later occupied by the Fultons, the Hendersons, the Kerrs, the Thomsons and latterly in 1906 by the Fleming family, whose last representative dwelt in it until his death around 1940. It was a two-storied structure which also had a sunken basement and its most famous owner, Mr. john Henderson, is reported to have made some changes to it 'though its original form was not greatly altered'. Finally deserted, it was used by our local villagers as a place to celebrate the end of the war in Europe in May 1945. It was to be demolished soon afterwards.

55 For long a venue of the Lanarkshire and Renfrewshire Hunt Park House was occupied, from 1839 to 1867, by Mr. John Henderson of Park, Esq., a celebrated Christian philanthropist who founded the National Bible Society of Scotland in 1860, the Duke of Argyll being that organization's first president and Mr. Henderson its first chairman. Of a charitable nature Mr. Henderson is credited with spending thirty to forty thousand pounds a year on 'good causes' whilst living in this building. First mentioned in 1496 its surrounding estate measured 551 acres in extent in 1905, and in the early 1930s it was obtained by the Department of Agriculture for Scotland as the location of a thirty plus smallholding scheme. These attractive looking little dwelling houses vanished (with a few exceptions) one by one as 'Erskine new township' expanded on this old estate's area from 1969-70 onwards.

Park House Inchinnan (First Meet of the Season)

56 Also built around 1780 the stables of Park House originally formed a square around a central court. Much reduced by demolition earlier this century they finally consisted of three sections of which a two-storied block – long used as a farmer's store – was by far the most striking part. Behind this edifice was to one side an open roofed barn which was attached to a long unoccupied cottage. A smaller ground-story building slightly to the north of it also constituted a surviving fragment. Forever a place for the young – and not so young – of our village to explore, yet again for the umpteenth time: all of these structures were demolished in February 1979 and today in Erskine the large 'Riverpark' apartment block that faces towards that private housing scheme's entry road from Park Drive substantially marks out the locality of this now gone stone-constructed complex.

57   A view of the Park Estate's stables block as they were seen after 1945 from the hillside behind them. A former attraction of their grounds was a small round pool which boasted of a little 'island' in its middle. Once a delightful feature to view with the demise of Park House this tiny ornamental pond soon fell to decay and for many years it lay totally untended and filled with stale greenish water that was invaded with all sorts of the most unwelcome growths and weeds. It finally vanished in 1981. Today its site still survives in its remaining trees only some feet from the playground of the 1981 opened St. Anne's primary school. Erskine's St. Berna-dette's Church which was officially opened in April 1987 also almost casts its shadow over its site. The stables area was usually explored by the curious – in pre-Erskine days – during the long evenings of the summer and autumn months.

58   Park Estate's fondly remembered rural crossroads lay 150 yards to the west of 'Bob Hamilton's smallholding'. Found where four little estate lanes converged 'in the middle of nowhere' locally speaking its accompanying vistas were to be admired irrespective of whether they were merely a field's length away or beyond the nearby river Clyde. Overlooked by six tall trees – now alas! all cut down – their very existence added majestically to the scenescape that they were already part of. Gradually surrounded by Erskine housing from mid-1978 onwards there was, at this now considerably changed but still existing crossroads, from about 1981 until near the end of 1996, a rounded stone pillar that was set upon a plinth, hence the 'monument area' name in Erskine. For long this relic had formed one of the two gateposts guarding the entry to the little lane that now leads onwards to the playground of the 1974 officially opened Park Mains High School.

59 A view uphill to and beyond the Park Estate's 'crossroads' locality. Now covered with houses and their serving roadways this vista shows this whole area in its original pre-1978 state. On the top of the hill the still extant line of trees is seen – but now without the residence of the late Mrs. Bain at its western end – that still overlooks both the Parksail and Park Mains parts of Erskine, whilst to the left, close to the camera, now the Mains Drive shopping centre stands. Just above the vanished trees at the crossroads Park Drive is today carried over the still extant walking lane by a short but sturdy roadway bridge, whilst at the top of the hill, opposite the site of Mrs.

Bain's former home, is the playground of the Barsail primary school, opened in August 1977. Mrs. Bain's old house which was occupied by more than one owner was from its building in 1935 till

its removal in 1977 a Park Estate 'landmark' in its own right.

60 Set above Barsail 'Gateside' was a coaching inn beside the Old Greenock Road when this highway was the sole Glasgow to Greenock route through our parish before it was redirected via 'The Red Smiddy' crossroads in the 1790s. Long disused as an inn by the 1900s Gateside was being used by the tenant of Park Mains Farm Mr. William Taylor, a celebrated Clydesdale horse breeder who died in May 1912 as a dwelling place for his farm hands. Despite having been removed around 1951, a small lower front part of it with its surviving windows filled in, remained as part of a smallholder's roadside wall, until the forming of Erskine's Newshot Drive in December 1980 finally removed all trace of it. According to the National Census returns of 1851 and 1861 'Gateside' was partly inhabited by the preachers who were in charge of Park Church then.

61 The Erskine Ferry's locality is held to mark the oldest fording place on the river Clyde westwards of the City of Glasgow and it was moved to its final operating position here early in the 18th century in consequence of a sandbank forming on the river at Old Kilpatrick. The ferry finally ceased business in the late evening of 2nd July 1971, only hours after the new Erskine High Bridge had been opened by Princess Anne, who had then crossed the river herself upon it. The deckman called out and I can still remember this cry, just before the ferry's – and my own – last ever crossing of the river Clyde: 'All you foreigners get off! Renfrewshire next stop!' The present writer considers himself to be one of the very first persons ever to have walked the complete length of Erskine's Barrhill Road and beyond to Inchinnan main village without this ferry being in existence.

62 A memorable vista of the Erskine Ferry's location as it was seen from its Old Kilpatrick village side before the First World War. Today the old Ferry Lodge – shown standing beside its former south bank stone service ramp – has been fully restored into a private residence. Previously there had been an attempt to demolish this building of 1860 because of its decayed condition. In 1854 an ancient canoe was discovered close by but, after it had been displayed for two years in the ferry house's garden, it had almost vanished – completely due to visiting relic hunters! It had measured 33 feet long, 4 feet broad and 3 feet 6 inches in depth. Also in 1855 the bones of a whale were discovered close to this ferry's precincts. In the earlier days of this century some people 'took the (tram) car to Renfrew and then walked through the woods to the Erskine Ferry'. Then on the winding Barrhill Road leading to it 'squirrels played on the trees that overshadowed it', a Glasgow area writer recorded in 1910.

Erskine Ferry, Old Kilpatrick.

63 Although today this view of the Erskine Ferry will look faintly more like the Renfrew Ferry vicinity to the newer generations, it records the fact that on the Old Kilpatrick side of the river Clyde there stood, from 1906 to 1930, the shipyard of Napier and Miller Ltd. Once obviously busy, the post-1918 world trade depression finally closed it down. For decades the Erskine Ferry was the end of many an 'outbound' Clydeside cyclist's 'run' as it was then one of their most popular destinations. But living close to the river crossing point had its downs as well as its ups, like for example in June 1880. A collection of 'partially' drunk men who had just used this ferry caused uproar in Old Kilpatrick village when they invaded its Free church's porch and – in the middle of a divine service - drowned out the minister's voice in the main kirk 'by filling its air with noise and oaths'.

64 A former pre-First World War Erskine Ferry craft. Although it may look antiquated now, for centuries the various ferry boats at Erskine – until 2nd July 1971 – were a vital link in the transport system in central western Scotland. In 1792, for example, foot passengers and horses and carts were its main users. Far more recently cars and lorries by the score, and other types of vehicles as well, used to wait for hours on end at this bottleneck – now of yeasteryear – to cross the 250 yards or so of the river Clyde to and from Old Kilpatrick village, which lay at its northern (Dunbartonshire) terminus. But there was also some compensation for the patient ones here, like viewing – despite the disruptions to the ferry crossings – some of the shipping that used the Clyde and admiring the attractive 1,300 foot high Kilpatrick Hills that overlooked this forever busy river Clyde vehicle transportation link.

65 The Erskine Ferry in 1961 in its 'final state' before – one decade later – it became a piece of Clydeside history. Its deck was usually covered with motor vehicles and foot passengers and cyclists found their accommodation on both sides. Pulled by chains across 'the water' it was a slow but memorable way to cross the Clyde. The building of a road bridge here had long been advocated – it was promised 'at an early date' in November 1933 for example – before work finally began in the late 1960s. Countless are the summer evenings when I strolled to and from the Erskine Ferry through the tranquil Park Estate during my continual walking expeditions to Old Kilpatrick and beyond. Since July 1971 walking across over the new high bridge has been a bit longer timewise, but the views from it are extensive, whilst beneath it lies Old Kilpatrick with its parish kirk of 1812 overlooking all that is close by.

ERSKINE FERRY RIVER CLYDE FROM SOUTH, OLD KILPATRICK   D 6467

66 Although I cannot give the date of its building 'The Ferry Inn' was described as 'a modern building' in 1917. In February 1916 Mr. Howard, the owner of the inn, reported that while visiting 'a town' he had heard the engine of a German Zeppelin airship passing over his head. During the First World War this building was used to house strangers visiting relatives who were being treated for war wounds in Erskine Hospital. 'The Ferry Inn', which was demolished in May 1976, was for long – and latterly as a private house – a 'standard' part of the scenescape hereabouts. The Erskine Ex-Servicemen's Hospital with grounds directly near this ferry also had a well-known handicraft shop, that sold basketwork and the like, often to the motorists who were wearily waiting for their place on this often busy – and even for the 1950s-1960s – completely outmoded ferrying service.

67   The scene just off what is now 'Erskine Beach' at the old Erskine Ferry, over which today the 180 feet high £11,000,000 Erskine Road Bridge towers. Just off here and located upon a rock is the Clyde Port Authority's beacon which is known as 'St. Patrick's Stone', because it is locally claimed that it was from here that St. Patrick, the patron saint of Ireland, was captured by pirates whilst peacefully fishing. It was they who took him to Ireland. Because of the strong river currents abounding at this 'beach', care has to be taken when bathing here. On countless occasions many fine Clyde-built vessel have passed by this 'shoreline', like the three 'Queen' liners the 'Lusitania', 'H.M.S. Hood' and 'H.M.S. Vanguard'. In the 19th century Lord Blantyre of Erskine House fought court actions against the Clyde Navigation Trust to keep his estate lands free from river works intrusions.

THE CLYDE AND OLD KILPATRICK HILLS AT ERSKINE FERRY   20A

68　When in 1804 Lord Blantyre purchased the original Northbarr Estate in our parish, he formed a little carriage bridge over the southern roadway to the Erskine Ferry to unite his two estates together. Long a feature here, it had due to its narrow dimensions by April 1914 become an obstacle for the traffic utilising the ferry and its demolition was proposed, one person saying that he doubted if it was ever used for 'traffic' even once a year and a landowner adding that it could 'go' if the side walls were made good. Still extant in December 1921 and May 1922, when its removal was again suggested, it has long since completely gone. The approaching lane on its Erskine Bridge side which – until quite recent years – had a lodge house near to its former locality, is 'with luck' still traceable. But in contrast the long abandoned service lane on its Erskine township side now lies heavily disguised within and beneath a powerful tangle of trees, bushes and weeds.

69 The 19th-century Southbar House stood within its surrounding wooded estate about a mile west of the Broomlands near 'the back road to Bishopton'. Constructed in 1842-1846 it suffered fire damage in February 1879 and finally burnt out in an accidental blaze in June 1921, during which a group of trapped firemen had to escape from the property by climbing out of one of its room windows. A considerable amount of this dwelling's furnishings were rescued during this terrible event and the estate workers toiled late into the evening to assist with its emergency storage. Relatively soon afterwards a new house was founded near the site of the former building. In 1897 this estate had been sold by the Alexander of Ballochmyle family to Mr. Robert Sutherland whose grandson, Lord Strachan, laid the foundation stone of our new parish church at Greenhead Farm in November 1966.

70 A rare view from 'The Glasgow Bulletin' newspaper showing the south side of the 1840s Southbar House. When the 1879 fire occured at this mansion, great crowds showed up to view the damaged building and earlier during this drama miners from the nearby Southbar Colliery hurriedly came to enquire if they could be of any assistance. Like Park House a mile or so away this residence was in the past visited by the Lanarkshire and Renfrewshire Hunt. From 1947 to 1986 the lands of Southbar Estate were used as a cattle breeding station by the Ministry of Agriculture and I can recall that whilst taking the occasional stroll through this property, I found close to the modern Southbar House some awfully big bulls, most fortunately tied up to stop them from wandering about! This estate, which was a Maxwell family property for three hundred years till about 1785, has had a lengthy local history.

71   Seen here from the south and long the base for a local smithy – hence its name – 'The Red Smiddy' probably came into existence in the 1790s when the main Glasgow to Greenock road was re-lined so as to avoid some of the steep hills that were upon its course, especially within the parish of Erskine. For decades merely a plain crossroads the Red Smiddy roundabout was founded here in 1938 to stop the growing number of vehicle accidents at this highway junction. As Renfrewshire's Chief Constable had proposed it, it was known for some time afterwards as 'Robertson's roundabout'. The now gone Red Smithy forge building was still here around 1960. Half a mile north of this crossroads on the Old Greenock Road is the 'Paisley Road Head', most likely named so because this is where the Paisley-Barnsford ferry road would meet the original Glasgow to Greenock highway within our parish before the new late-18th century highway to Greenock was formed through its more level central parts.

72   Although a much less celebrated highway toll house than the one at 'the bridges', the Barnsford Toll none the less lasted 'as a going concern' for many years. For ages placed at a quiet road junction its locality is now almost overshadowed by a factory looking across to it from the now adjoining 'Inchinnan Business Park'. Within the last two years the whole area to the west of it and of the Red Smiddy has been proposed – amidst loud local opposition – as the scene of a gigantic industrial estate. In 1919 on this same area there was a proposal to build upon it the 'new town' of Georgetown 'right away' to the Fullwood Bridge near Linwood. Huge in concept and population this town was planned as an enlargement of the Glasgow area's shell filling factory's village of Georgetown, which then stood less than a mile west of the Barnsford Toll. But this new post-1918 'Georgetown' was never to come to fruition. Around September 1932 an Episcopal mission station – 'no bigger than a car garage' – was opened near this 'Toll' and this was to be its feature for some years.

73　Set rurally at the south-western corner of our parish the Barnsford Bridge (which is incorrectly named on this postcard) replaced, in 1793, a privately-owned Black Cart ferry that operated upon this site, the Burgh of Paisley paying £100 towards its building costs. Despite being 'improved' in 1909 it remained – even from that date – a narrow, weak, oldfashioned structure without a foot pavement. A late-1930s scheme to replace it collapsed with the events of 1939. Latterly unable to cope with the traffic demands of Erskine some two miles to the north, this pretty little structure was finally demolished by the end of 1986, within two or three months of its successor having been opened beside it. Just north-east of here – since the mid-1970s – the ever expanding 'Inchinnan Business Park' has 'grown up', and most recently a huge traffic roundabout was completed on 'our' side of the modern Barnsford Bridge to improve the vehicle routes that serve this large Industrial Estate.

Inchinnan Bridge near Renfrew.

74 Standing close to the original Barnsford Bridge, Walkinshaw House with its pleasure grounds was within the parish of Renfrew, although its estate once included a fair part of Inchinnan parish land. Erected in 1792 after the plans of Robert Adam its strange triangular-shaped bulk – said by some to be of a unique design – survived until its demolition in the 1920s. Earlier the Walkinshaw Pit had undermined this mansion house's foundations leaving its walls both cracked and weakened and in 1914 it was stated that the manager of this mine was utilising this edifice as his residence. Writing around 1700 the Lanarkshire and Renfrewshire historian William Hamilton of Wishaw recorded that the estate could be reached from the river Clyde by boating along the Black Cart River. Set close to its site and considerably out of repair are today the substantial remains of this estate's former stables block.

75   Georgetown village, which was set on the quiet B790 Inchinnan to Bridge of Weir road, was hurriedly founded in 1915 to house some of the workers of the Glasgow area's great shell making factory of Georgetown, which was named after David Lloyd George, the Minister of Munitions and later British Prime Minister, who opened this factory in December 1915. Standing in a countryside area immediately beside the Glasgow to Gourock railway two miles north-west of Paisley, this little hamlet consisted totally of wooden houses that were mainly demolished in 1939, when even its sub-post office was closed down. A few of these houses remained 'in situ' until they were all finally removed around 1972. If unromantic in purpose, Georgetown village's wartime factory's site was equally unfortunate, as it covered the area of a working pre-1914 city of Glasgow refuge dumping site.

The Bungalows, Georgetown.

76 The Georgetown Shell Filling Factory (No. 4), which had employed many thousands of workers, closed in 1918 and soon afterwards its equipment was disposed of by public sale. Its manufacturing buildings were dismantled leaving only their concrete flooring visible upon the 250 acre site. In 1939 this area was included in the new Bishopton Ordnance Factory. Previously its confines had been planted with fir trees that in 1929 were described as being '18 inches high' and which are now considerably taller! By the late 1920s the former shell workers houses were in a shocking state of repair and the village continually declined in both population and housing stock until it finally vanished completely in the early 1970s, its railway station having being closed down in 1959. Yet, despite all of this, 'Georgetown' is still referred to – more than 25 years later – as if this little place still existed.